SAINT ANTHONY of PADUA

A VOICE FROM HEAVEN

ANTON ROTZETTER

Translated by Sharon Therese Nemeth

ST. ANTHONY MESSENGER PRESS

Cincinnati, Ohio

Cover and book design by Mark Sullivan
Cover photo by Gene Plaisted, O.S.C.

This book was first published in German, as *Antonius von Padua*, copyright ©
1996, Verlag Butzon & Bercker, Kevalaer, Germany.

Library of Congress Cataloging-in-Publication Data

Rotzetter, Anton.
  [Antonius von Padua. English]
  Saint Anthony of Padua : the voice from heaven / Anton Rotzetter ;
translated by Sharon Therese Nemeth.
      p. cm.
  ISBN 0-86716-492-1 (alk. paper)
  1. Anthony, of Padua, Saint, 1195-1231. 2. Christian
saints--Italy--Biography. I. Title.
  BX4700.A6R6813 2004
  282'.092--dc22

                                        2003025699

Introduction

I HAVE LONG WANTED TO dedicate a book to Saint Anthony of Padua, whose name I bear. This welcome opportunity came about in 1995, the 800th anniversary of the celebration of Saint Anthony's birth.

But what does a person's birth really mean? Instead of birth we sometimes say that one "first sees the light of the world." Is birth therefore the moment of opening our eyes for the first time and recognizing the world around us? Is it the passage from the darkness of the womb into the light of being?

Or might it actually be just the reverse? Could birth be the moment when the world first takes note of us? In which we are recognized? When we step out of the shadows into the light of the world and are perceived by others?

In the case of Saint Anthony, one is tempted to see the second definition as the meaning of "birth." For as important as Saint Anthony's biological birth was, the more important date was in the fall of 1222, when Anthony took his comrades by surprise and spoke publicly for the first time. Prior to this moment, Saint Anthony was merely a shadow in a hermitage and revealed little or none of his character to his friends. Before this time not much notice had been taken of him, but from then on no one was able to forget him as his name traveled from mouth to mouth, from place to place, from country to country.

His earthly existence was like a shooting star in the heavens: he would not even be granted a full ten years to light the way home for others. On June 13, 1231 the star was extinguished outside the city of Padua, at the same time to rise again in a completely different way.

Therefore I'm not able to tell the story of my patron saint in a linear fashion: there are no straight lines between birth and death, just as there aren't between earthly and eternal life. There are only cracks and fissures. I hope to show this as well through my telling of his story.

January 1995

1:
The "Birth" of Saint Anthony

IN SAN MERCURIALE IN
Forli, a city near Bologna, several young men, among them
Franciscans and Dominicans, were ordained to priesthood at
the end of September 1222. To the shock of those in attendance, it was discovered that there was no one present to celebrate the occasion with an oration worthy of the event.

The traditional interpretation of the story, which
describes this as the sermon held during the actual ordination, is problematic. First, the bishop himself would have
been called on in this situation, and secondly, the oldest
biography from the year 1232 used the word *exhortatio* to
describe the task to be carried out. However, the *exhorte*, as

we know particularly from Franciscan sources, was a spoken act outside of the liturgical celebration, and it was possible for a common lay brother to perform. Thirdly, mention was made of a *minister loci*, a Franciscan who was responsible for the local community of brothers of Forli in a function that would later be called *guardian*. As such it would also be his duty to arrange the celebration, which included, among other things, a fitting *exhorte*. These reasons would seem to indicate this was a post-ceremony celebration held in a brotherly circle.

Getting back to the event itself, the guardian was shocked to find out that no one in attendance was prepared to give a speech that would provide the fitting expression to the occasion. He searched among those present for someone to take over this task. But everyone he asked declined. The renowned preachers, the Dominicans, refused to speak because of their sincere conviction that it was necessary to meditate before giving a sermon. The Franciscans declined because they considered themselves lacking the necessary training to do the event justice. Acting more out of uncertainty and exasperation than out of reason and clarity, the guardian ordered Brother Anthony, who had come with a group from the nearby hermitage of Montepaolo, to speak.

Anthony had lived an unassuming life in the hermitage. His existence had been plain and simple as was fitting for a Friars Minor. He was a disciple who followed the way of Saint Francis. According to Saint Francis' rule for the hermitage, he had, like everyone else, served as a "mother," which meant carrying out daily tasks such as cooking, cleaning and begging for alms, as well as listening when another brother needed a patient ear in times of trouble. And then, after a time, he retreated for a longer period in solitude to contemplate and find shelter in the mystery of God. If needed, he too entrusted his own worries to another brother's care or the "mother" in whom he placed his trust. This is the cycle that marked the life in the hermitages and left its impression on Anthony.

How was this brother, who had not attracted attention before, unless it had been because of his lack of words, now supposed to find the right words at the right time? Nevertheless, Anthony obeyed. And those in attendance were astonished by what flowed from the lips of the one who had up to now been silent. As his fellow brothers listened they recognized many gifts of Saint Anthony: a vast knowledge of the Scriptures; a sense of their intrinsic meaning for the present; a fresh language with words that sounded as if they had just been created; awe-inspiring and heartening perspectives; quotations from Saint Augustine, Saint Jerome, Saint Gregory and many others; a clear structure, concise logic, a unique expressive ability.

Everyone was speechless as they listened, and their mouths dropped open in disbelief. Anthony, in that moment, became the person we recognize today: the speaker, evangelist, preacher, theologian and, to use the words of Saint Francis, one who gives "spirit and life."

According to the oldest biography Anthony is the "*old tonans,*" or one who sounds a pure tone, loudly and clearly. This tone is a voice given to him by heaven. While the etymological origin of the name, "old tonans," is not linguistically correct (the Greek *tonos* actually means to stretch), the word itself refers to vocal or musical sounds. So the inherent significance was accurate. At the last examination of the remains of the saint in 1981, it was revealed that in addition to the skeleton, including the jawbone, the tongue as well as the entire vocal organs remained fully intact.

However this might be perceived, one thing is certain: in 1222 a great preacher was born, and the world received Anthony, a voice from heaven.

2:
The Humble Beginnings

Childhood and Education

Near the cathedral of Lisbon, the house of Anthony's birth can still be seen. Fernando, as his parents, Martin Alfonsi and his wife Maria, named him, was born here on August 15, 1195. As the child of a knight in the service of King Alfonso II, Anthony was one of the privileged few, and therefore he was allowed to attend the cathedral school. There he was instructed in the "trivium" (grammar, dialectics and rhetoric) and the "quadrivium" (arithmetic, astronomy, geometry and music.)

We know nothing about his childhood. However, there are many legends and stories that have been passed from century to century in which Fernando is shown in a dazzling light. Some stories say that whatever Fernando looked at became colorful and whatever he touched was healed. Most stories of his childhood attempt to reflect God's closeness to him. But mostly these fantastical stories belong to the realm of the imagination, for Fernando was no different than any other child.

The Augustinians

The oldest life story of Saint Anthony, however, tells something about the awakening of the young Fernando's sexuality. Fernando sensed this aspect of his person as something threatening, or even evil. He believed that he could escape it through flight to the cloister. Such a motive of flight may seem quite difficult to understand today, but it corresponds to a time strongly marked by dualism, which required one to bid the evil world (or physical world) farewell.

So at the age of fifteen, Fernando entered the novitiate of the Canons Regular of San Vicente near Lisbon, an order that followed the rule of Saint Augustine. He did not find the serenity he was seeking there. Fernando was unable to focus, because his companions and friends often came to visit and spirit him away to noisy festivities. Seeking out more solitude, Fernando moved to the cloister at Coimbra, the capital of Portugal at the time, where the order had a world-famous center for studies.

At Coimbra, Fernando had access to excellent professors and one of the best libraries of his day. Here he laid the foundation for his broad theological knowledge, reflected later in his sermons and books. Above all, he learned a theological method he would later master with great skill. This skill Fernando mastered was his ability to transcend the words of a text. While not remaining fixed on the words on the page, Fernando crossed the threshold of the text and searched for its practical application and its implication for the future.

While in Coimbra at the Canons Regular of San Vicente, it has been argued that Fernando also became a priest. Though sources do not say explicitly where and when Fernando became a priest, it is understood that whoever entered the Canons Regular would be ordained as a priest and take up pastoral ministry. The entire education at the Canons Regular was directed toward the aim of the priestly vocation. Thus it is probable that Fernando was ordained a priest as soon as the church law and circumstances allowed for it, even before he became a Franciscan in the year 1220.

The Franciscans

On January 16, 1220 six Franciscans were killed in Morocco because they had provoked the Muslims with their aggressive missionary work. Berard, Peter, Accurs, Adjute, Otto and Vitalis had ignored the instructions of Saint Francis, who had wanted the brothers to live without aggression and in peace among the Muslims, even being subjugated to them. Francis taught his followers that they should simply bear witness to their faith as Christians and avoid conflict. Many at the time believed if Berard and his companions had done this nothing would have happened to them, for during that same time period there were a number of Christians who lived peacefully with Muslims in Morocco. Pedro, the brother of the Portuguese King Alfonso II, had even settled there and maintained friendly relations with the Emir-el-mimenin, the "Lord of the Faithful" or Miramolin, as he is called in our tradition.

Nevertheless, Pedro secretly brought the bodies of these Franciscan "martyrs" for the faith out of the country and then to Coimbra. At the cloister church of the monastery where Fernando lived, they were buried in the vault normally reserved for the kings of Portugal. Fernando was shaken so deeply that Berard and his brothers were willing to die for their belief in Jesus Christ that after painful hours of contemplation and struggle, he decided to become a Franciscan himself.

However, it must be said that this was not Fernando's first exposure to the Franciscans. In fact, since 1217 the Franciscans had settled just outside of Coimbra in "Sant Antonio de Olivães." Here they were able to live their solitary life of devotion for longer periods of time before setting off on their preaching tours. The Franciscans undoubtedly knocked on the gate of the Augustinian cloister more than once to beg for a piece of bread or something else to eat. On many such occasions Fernando had the opportunity for personal contact with the brothers. It is often assumed that it was during these conversations with the brothers that Fernando first became inspired by the words and spirituality of Francis, and his own intentions to become a Franciscan matured steadfastly in his heart.

To be able to enter the Franciscan Order, he needed the permission of his own order. It was given to him, though granted with reservation. As one source tells us, he was considered a promising candidate for the position of Prior at the cloister. The sources tell of another unnamed Augustinian, whose disagreement with the decision was quite vehement, and who suffered as a result of the leave-taking.

From the Franciscan perspective, the situation was much easier. In the summer of 1220 there was not yet a novitiate period, which first became obligatory with the proclamation of Honorious III in September 1220. Additionally, there were not yet any special conditions for acceptance in the order. At the time Fernando wished to join, it was enough that the candidate was passionate about God, wanted to follow the Scriptures literally, divided his property among the poor, was Catholic and, in the case of Fernando Martini Alfonsi of Lisbon, had the permission of his previous Order.

Once permissions were granted, the Franciscans pulled the simple robe over Fernando, and he was from that point on a Franciscan. Unlike most Franciscans, who kept their Christian-given name, Fernando took on a new name. Fernando chose to call himself Anthony, after the name of the Franciscan settlement. At the time he wished to "fall into namelessness," or in keeping with his humble nature, to be anonymous.

One might say that the sole motive for this radical change of place was Anthony's desire for martyrdom. Though Anthony had admired the Franciscans during his stay with the Augustinians, it was not until he witnessed the burial of the Franciscan martyrs that he finally made the decision to unconditionally emulate those who were killed on behalf of Jesus Christ. Thus he set off for Morocco in that summer of 1220 in order to serve as a witness for Christ, or even, he hoped, to die for him. But malaria forced him to change his direction and head back to Portugal. En route, a violent storm drove his ship to the shores of Sicily.

The place where Anthony's ship washed ashore and where he stayed on the island are not known. Various localities such as the "Bay of Saint Anthony," a hermitage near Messina, Cefalù and Vizzini, San Mauro di Castlemonte and others vie for some of the fame that would later surround Anthony. We only know that he found brotherly care somewhere by Franciscans and remained there for a long time affected by illness, lethargy and passivity.

The Principle of Passivity

One of the key points or aspects in Anthony's spiritual journey came during his illness, when, for the first time in his life, Anthony was forced to be a passive recipient of God's call. At no other point in Anthony's life did he relinquish his free will to God. In fact, wasn't he the one who at the age of fifteen decided to become an Augustinian in order to escape from the evil world? Wasn't he the one who then decided to escape to Coimbra when Lisbon became too hectic? Wasn't it he who had asserted his will in order to become a Franciscan? And didn't he do it only because he, Anthony, wanted to force the cause of martyrdom upon himself? Hadn't he been the one who up to now had always held the scepter in his hand? But where was God in this view of life? Anthony, for the first time in his life, came face to face with this realization, and finally he succumbed to God's call, which in his case came in the form of malaria and a storm at sea. Anthony was finally rendered powerless and was unable to make a decision based solely on his own needs. Anthony was now at the mercy and hands of God and willing to do only what he was called to do.

Another Anthony, Antonio Rosmini, who lived from 1797 to 1855, formulated the spiritual perspective of the "principle of passivity." Antonio Romini described a "behavioral rule by which the Christian through his own initiative gives priority to humility by stepping back into seclusion in order not to disturb God's work through activity.

Nevertheless, he must be prepared to be at God's disposal, prepared to leave his hermitage and prepared to dedicate himself to all the works which answer the will of God." It is certain that what is described here as a general principle of Christian life was reflected in Anthony's behavior in the thirteenth century. The early sources do not leave any doubts open. Even Julian of Speyer wrote: "Anthony was filled with glowing fervor for the House of God. Yet through godly intervention his soul was confronted with emptiness. From then on he lost the desire to be driven by his inner pride. He gave himself over in a more perfect way, filled with trust, to the mystery of God, and he waited in great openness until God would give him a clear sign."

The Pentecost Chapter of Mats in Assisi (1221)
How it was possible for Anthony to take part in the internal Franciscan gathering, the Pentecost Chapter of Mats in Assisi (so named because there was no place for the 3,000 friars to sleep but on mats), while ill remains a mystery. We have to assume that he simply let himself be taken along. We also do not know anything about the route he took there with his brothers. Two places in Calabria—Pizzo and San Marco Argentano—were known to have served as places of repose for the saint along the way.

During Anthony's time, Pentecost Chapters were still great days of celebration and community for all the brothers.

The Chronicles of the Friars Minor Brothers, Jordan of Giano and Thomas Eccleston reported that 3,000, possibly even 5,000, brothers gathered below the Porziuncola. The presence of the Cistercian Cardinal, Rainer Capocci, a number of bishops and representatives of other orders added a particular significance to the gathering. The brothers slept out in the open and met during the day, communing under especially set-up shaded areas. The inhabitants of Assisi brought food and drink, in fact so much so that the chapter had to be extended for two days in order that the contributions would not go to waste. Francis was the great spiritual authority here, even though he no longer carried out the office of general minister. At the opening ceremony he read the Scriptures and preached on the theme: "Praise be the Lord, my God, who guides my hands in battle." When he was not speaking, Francis sat at the feet of the Vicar General, Brother Elias, and tugged at his robe every time he had something to say. Elias bent down to listen, and then straightening up said: "Brothers, the brother has something to say." Francis was the absolute embodiment of the brother; it was no longer even necessary to mention his name.

We do not know whether or not Anthony met Francis that day. But we do know that he did not draw attention to himself in any way, and was recognized as a great man of silence at the chapter. He had nothing to say, nor did he have a desire to speak. Thus his education, intelligence, special charisma, as well as his priestly office, remained completely hidden from view. When the brothers were divided into new groups at the end of the chapter, little interest was shown in him. When the brothers were sent out to different regions, Anthony remained on the sidelines until he asked Brother Graziano, the person responsible for Upper Italy, or Romagna as it was called at the time, to take him along to a little hermitage near Montepaolo.

According to sources written almost one hundred years later, Brother Graziano asked whether or not Anthony was a priest, to which Anthony expressed an affirmation. Brother Graziano, with this news, agreed to take him along. It is important to point out that Brother Graziano's question of Anthony's priesthood in 1221 was incongruous, because the community of Saint Francis was most decidedly a brotherhood. There were a few priests, but it was not the norm. The brothers were first and foremost brothers, and whoever was a priest joined the established way of life. Additionally, before 1224, the year in which the pope allowed the Friars Minor the privilege of using the transportable altar, there were not yet Eucharistic celebrations in Franciscan hermitages. For Brother Graziano to ask this question leaves one to wonder, what had Anthony said or done to perhaps reveal his scholarly position?

Montepaolo

Despite Anthony's admission that he was indeed a priest, accounts of Saint Anthony's life show that he was called on to be ordained to the priesthood for reasons of pastoral ministry at the hermitage of Montepaolo. Though there is little knowledge today about why or how it came to be that Anthony again went through the ordination process or why he was not forthcoming with the information of his own priesthood in the first place, we can be quite sure that Anthony had not given the slightest indication of his education and his ecclesiastical function (including priesthood) to his brothers, with the exception of Brother Graziano. This applies not only to the Pentecost Chapter of 1221, but also to his entire time at Montepaolo.

Anthony's humility had no end and despite his priesthood, he still occupied himself with the most menial of tasks such as washing, cleaning and cooking. It is part of the Franciscan way of life: whether one is educated or illiterate, priest or layman, no one is exempt from the menial tasks of daily life.

Anthony's time in Montepaolo did not last even one and a half years. But it would be a crucial period in two ways: he would now finally be able to grow into Franciscan spirituality, and he would revise his original motive for becoming a Franciscan—from martyrdom to servitude. While martyrdom was certainly an impressive motive, it was not decisive for the Franciscan way of life, or the life Anthony sought, which was based on Francis' teaching. Instead, Anthony sought to do what was instructed of him as a Franciscan. This meant: following the words of Mark in Chapter 10 by giving up everything and living in poverty with the poor; acting as an itinerate preacher as directed in Matthew 10; spreading the Good News as a poor man to the poor; practicing brotherly love in a simple, clear framework by being a brother to others; listening to others and being sensitive to their needs; embracing the whole world and realizing that everything that exists, exists as a brother and sister; and making the choice for God as Jesus showed us by receiving, listening, reading, celebrating and witnessing.

It was in Montepaolo that Anthony embraced these teachings. He lived in silence, in contemplation and in radical openness to the mystery of God. Besides all of the daily tasks to be performed, which also served to nurture a simple heart and brotherliness, Anthony knew only one thing: God was present.

This life of silence ended abruptly in September 1222, and once more God called on Anthony, the passive recipient, to begin his oration at the ordination of priests in Forli.

3:
A Voice from Heaven

THE ASTONISHING AND fascinating sermon in Forli had immediate consequences. Anthony's gift of oration had caught the attention of the public too powerfully, and he could not simply be allowed to return to Montepaolo again.

The Itinerate Preacher

Immediately following the sermon in Forli, Anthony was given the duties of itinerate preaching by the Friars Minor. He would thus exchange the peacefulness of the hermitage for the restless life of one who travels from one place to another in order to bring people to God and the Church. Fundamentally, every Franciscan is an itinerate preacher who does not need a special assignment to carry out this work (Francis himself insisted on this in his rule when he described a sermon that everyone could and should use as a model). Nevertheless, Anthony's gift was too impressive to be ignored or subject to the confines of a model or rule.

In Forli, Anthony was called on only to perform an *exhorte*, a form of lay sermon recognized by the church. Instead, Anthony gave a sermon that not only called others to repent and to worship God, but also attempted to interpret the life of Christ. This sermon made it clear to all present: Anthony was a scholar. Moreover, Anthony was someone who knew the teachings of the church more than anyone else in the order and who kept to the rules of clerical preaching. And there before everyone, it was revealed that he was indeed a priest too. Anthony was then given the official directive to bring together his special gift of ecclesiastical preaching and the itinerate life of a Franciscan with a reminder of the directive that all Franciscans use Francis' original model sermon.

The Cathari

A further observation can help to shed more light on Francis' directive. In Middle and Upper Italy, but also and primarily in Southern France, many feared the false doctrine of the Cathari, which was becoming more widespread. Members of this group opposed the official Church and demanded a more "pure and spiritual church." The Cathari rejected all earthly things. They admonished the corruptions of the church authorities. They abandoned the sacraments, believing the sacraments placed too much importance on the material. The Cathari also did not believe that God came to Earth in a physical way. Their belief was that a pure spirit and soul must be kept pure from contact with the material world.

This teaching had a great following, mainly because of the fascinating, radical way in which the Cathari practiced it, and because the accusations the Cathari made against the rich and powerful Church were based on real failings. Entire regions and cities turned to them. In Spoleto and other places they even set up a church-alternative organizational structure, which included their own "bishops" and their own rites. As a result, there were many public disturbances and violent confrontations. For instance, we know from the life of Saint Aldebrand, who was the Bishop of Rimini from 1222–1228, that there was a revolt of the Cathari in Rimini. Fleeing the city, Aldebrand was just barely able to escape with his life. The entire city was under Cathari control.

Saint Francis' directive and models on teaching, therefore, were not intended to limit scholastic thought; they were intended to limit a scholarly theologian's pride, and thus the possible heresy or gross misinterpretations that can grow out of such pride.

First Preaching Phase: Italy 1222–1224

Anthony seemed to be the ideal man who, with his powerful words and captivating speaking gift, could take on the large task of bringing the Cathari back to the church. Untiringly, he traveled and preached extensively. He was later dubbed the "Hammer of Heresy" for his powerful sermons. Anthony did not go about his work timidly, but unlike his former inspirations, the five Franciscan martyrs who preached aggressively among nonbelievers, Anthony spoke on behalf of the Church peacefully and with warmth and understanding.

He began in Rimini where the situation was critical. In the beginning, Anthony had difficulty getting the people to listen. It was only after some time that he suddenly achieved an unexpected breakthrough when he was able to convert Bononillus, an avid follower of the Cathari for thirty years of his life. According to the oldest sources, his function was apparently a bishop of the Cathari. This conversion, then, marked Anthony's uncanny ability to persuade and convert the seemingly stubborn Cathari.

From Rimini, Anthony progressed further along the seaside to Ravenna. He preached and carried out his mission in Bologna and Milan, and even went as far as Vercelli in Piedmont, where he met the famous theologian Thomas Gallus. Most of the time, however, he traveled through Romagna, or the entire area of Upper Italy.

The Second Preaching Phase: Southern France 1224–1227

In 1224 Anthony was sent to Southern France, the stronghold of the Cathari, where the church's yearlong crusade against them had proved futile and useless. Many hoped that Anthony might be able to curtail the violence through his powerful gift of oration.

He crossed over the entire region in three years. The most important stations along the road of his untiring mission as itinerate preacher were: Arles, the meeting place for the Franciscans; Montpellier, the military center of the Catholic crusaders; Toulouse, the center of the Cathari; Le Puy, where Anthony was still guardian; Bourges, where he participated at a Synod; and Limoges, where huge numbers of people gathered to hear him. In the meantime churches had become too small to meet the needs of all those who gathered to hear Anthony speak and he was asked to find alternative venues to accommodate the large crowds—such as marketplaces, fields and even cemeteries.

The Chapter of Arles in the Fall of 1224

On September 29, 1224, the feast day of Saint Michael, the Franciscans in southern France came together in Arles for a voluntary meeting, or chapter, which was presented in the Rule of 1223. Four years later, Thomas of Celano noted:

> Also in attendance at this chapter was
> Brother Anthony, whose mind the Lord

opened so that he understood the Scriptures and spoke about Jesus to all the people with words sweeter than honey. While he was preaching with the deepest fervor and complete devotion to the brothers on the passage: "Jesus of Nazareth, King of the Jews," Brother Monald looked over to the entrance of the house where the brothers were meeting. There, he saw with his own eyes blessed Francis floating in the air, his hands outspread as if on a cross, giving his blessings to the brothers. And it was evident that everyone was filled with the comfort of the Holy Spirit, and the blessed joy they sensed truly made real what they had heard about the manifestation and presence of the glorious Father. (Works, 1999)

The effect of Anthony's powerful oration was echoed here not only in the words of Thomas of Celano, but also in the impression Anthony made on the people in attendance. The presence of Jesus, the suffering king, was burned into their minds so deeply that one of the brothers believed to see Francis there with outspread arms, as one crucified, an image later immortalized by Giotto. The representation of Francis' body as a cross became even more meaningful when one knows that shortly before, on the Feast of the Elevation of the Cross, September 14, Francis had received the stigmata. Perhaps in this event we are able to see more than anywhere else the special link between Francis and Anthony: Francis' physical manifestation was brought about through Anthony's gift of expression. This account was especially valuable because it was written during Anthony's lifetime and therefore even before his canonization.

The Synod of Bourges on November 30, 1225

While the previously described chapters were an internal gathering of Franciscans, the Synod of Bourges was an ecclesiastical event. At the gathering, which was called by Simon de Sully, the Archbishop of Bourges, the focal point of discussion was the state of the church in southern France and what should be done to solve problems that had arisen. In addition to the nuncio sent by Pope Honorious III, six archbishops, approximately one hundred bishops, prelates and the superiors of various orders took part, as well as a significant number of earls and princes, among them Amanry of Montfort and Raymund of Toulouse. However, it was not pure, selfless interest that brought these men together; rather, it was the hope of expanding sovereign territory. In addition, at the center of discussion was the implementation of measures to outlaw and expel the Cathari from various provinces. With the Cathari evacuated, this would leave several powerful positions available in the Cathari region, and many men at the Synod were hoping to be able to fill the power vacuum. Archbishop Simon de Sully was no exception. He too had desires for such a position.

Anthony was also a member of the synod. He recognized quickly the two-fold intention of the participants. In his sermon, which he delivered in front of the synod, he spoke directly to the archbishop with a bit of sarcasm, but mostly sincerity: "Now I speak to you horned one." The synod could have easily interpreted this statement as an address to the devil himself but because Anthony spoke directly toward the man with the miter, there was no doubt to whom Anthony was speaking (Works, 1999).

Despite the obvious accusation, the archbishop was affected by Anthony's words and felt deep remorse. From thence onward, the synod progressed without the usual practice of distributing power and haggling, and in the end the archbishop confessed his sins to Anthony and went on to live in greater devotion to God.

Church Critic

Anthony was notorious for being a relentless church critic. His words, chosen wisely, were never meant to sugarcoat or euphemize. Anthony never allowed the mistakes of the church to be hidden or kept from the people. He realized that much of the trouble with the Cathari movement was not the people of the movement, but what they were ultimately opposed to: corruption in the Catholic Church. Again and again he called the offenders in the Church by name. Below are a few examples of Anthony's reprimands:

> But the Bishop of our day is like Balaam: he sits upon the donkey that sees the angel, but he himself cannot see it! He is an incompetent fool, a disgraceful Bishop. With his bad example he plunges the benevolent community of the faithful first into sinfulness, and then into hell. With his stupidity and ignorance he confuses the people! With his stinginess he devours the population! I say such a man sits on the donkey and does not see the angel! He sees the devil, who wants to plunge him into hell! But the simple people, the people who truly believe and act for what is right—these people see the angel of great counsel. They love and recognize the Son of God. (Sermon I, 202)

> He who buys an ecclesiastical office is a villain! Like a thief in the night he steals and lays claim to what does not belong to him; the sheep that belong to the Lord, he makes his own. He is a thief, hiding in the clothing of holiness! He seizes the lamb, because he is a wolf! He robs those who are not careful of their virtue, and he kills their souls! (Sermon I, 263)

The Devil climbs the mountain. He goes to those who have reached the peak of honor. There he exults in the wind of vainglory and worldly pomp. The Devil fears two things most of all: the fire of love and the well-worn path of humility! (Sermon I, 268)

The day laborers and the Devil are bound to each other in friendship.

The prelate is told by the Devil to give me souls! The Devil and the earthly rulers do with the prelates what the wolves did to the fisherman of the Meontic swamps*: the wolves came to the house of the fishermen and did them no harm, as long as they received fish from them. But when the fishermen refused to give them fish, the wolves tore up the nets the fishermen laid out to dry. In this way the prelates of the Church give souls to the devil, and earthly rulers the goods of the Church, so that the nets of their business, their worldly transactions and ties of relationships, are not hindered or destroyed. (Sermon I, 269)

*Reference is made here to a story told by Aristotle.

The Third Preaching Phase: Italy 1227-1231

In 1227 Anthony returned to Upper Italy because the General Chapter had elected him to the office of provincial of Romagna. In addition to this office, he continued to carry out his itinerate preaching. He even ventured to the outermost borders of Italy to the area of Trieste, traveling to Istria, as well as Pula, Muggia, Porec, Cividale, Germona, Gorizia, Udine, Conegliano, Treviso, Venice, Trient, Riva, Verona, Bassano del Grappa, Milan, Como, Bienno in Val Camonica, Cremona, Brescia, Bregamo, Varese, Mantua, Ferrara and Padua, which ultimately became his home. Many other places also had the opportunity to experience Saint Anthony's fascinating oration. Already at this time he would occasionally make his pulpit the boughs of a tree. Whether or not this choice had a deeper significance for him is not known; what is known, however, is his deep love of God's nature, especially trees.

From a physical aspect alone, Anthony's life as an itinerate preacher was remarkable. As befits a Franciscan, Anthony traveled everywhere barefoot, just like Saint Francis who believed that one was not able to proclaim the Good News to the poor in the way of a rich man. Wherever Anthony went, huge throngs of people came to see him. Many believed they had finally found a man of the cloth on their side against the abuse of power by the powerful Church and the corruption and insatiability of rich society. They admired his straightforwardness, his unambiguous language. They believed him to be truly one of the people. (He was not always well-received and was sometimes the victim of verbal abuse during his travels.)

Despite various obstacles, excessive travel, wear on the body, not to mention the occasional dissident, Anthony continued to inspire people. But it was not his polemics alone that drew people to him. Anthony offered the people something they were desperately in search of—he offered them a deep understanding and knowledge of God and their relationship to God.

The following sermons reveal Anthony's simple rhetoric, which ultimately expressed to his followers the ever-elusive Incarnation of God.

> The bread of the angels is the milk of the infants. The angels shall make themselves small. The little ones shall come to nurse and be satisfied at the comforting bosom.
> (Sermon III, 5)

> The milk is good and its sight is pleasing.
> Just as Christ is.
> With his goodness
> he draws people to him,
> and even the angels
> yearn for the sight of him!
> (Sermon III, 5)

The fullness of time!
The day of salvation!
The year of grace!
Since the time Adam went astray
until the advent of Christ
there was nothing but
emptiness,
almost nothing,
but the Devil's devastation.
Days of pain
and infirmity,
years of affliction.
But now:
our days are full.
He fills them with his birth!
And from the fullness of these days
we have all received!
(Sermon III, 5)

You,
blessed Virgin,
may you be praised and glorified!
In the goodness of your house,
at your bosom,
we experience abundance!
In the past we were empty,
but today we are filled!

In the past we were feeble,
today we are whole;
In the past we were cursed,
today we are blessed!
(Sermon III, 5)

See the goodness!
See the paradise!
Come
You who are hungry,
You misers and usurers,
all of you
who love money more than God!
Come,
buy without money
buy without receiving anything in return,
the grain that the Virgin
brought forth today
from her granary,
her womb!
(Sermon III, 6)

What Son is this?
God.
The Son of God.
O much happier
than happy

are you,
who has a son
with God,
the Father!
How much honor
comes upon a poor, wretched woman
who has a son with a
mortal emperor!
And how much more honor
comes upon a Virgin
who with God the Father
has a son!
(Sermon III, 6)

From the father
the godly nature,
from the mother
the mortal one.
From the father,
divinity
from the mother,
human frailty.
Emmanuel:
God with us.
Who can then be
against us?
(Sermon III, 6)

Humanity
is the helmet.
Divinity
is the head
concealed
beneath.
Divinity
concealed beneath humanity.
Do not fear!
We will triumph!
For the armed God is with us!
(Sermon III, 6)

Wrapped in swaddling clothes.
and lying in a manger.
O poverty!
O humility!
The Lord of the Universe:
wrapped in swaddling clothes
The King of Angels:
lying in the stable.
Blush with shame,
you insatiable greed!
Waste away,
you human pride!
(Sermon III, 7)

The glorious Virgin,
an empress, our Queen,
like a coal
glowing with fire,
immersed in the Holy Spirit!
Like Sarah
God gives her
laughter.
From her
our laughter is born.
Christ is born.
Laughter is born,
thus we are able to laugh.
Let us rejoice together with the blessed
Virgin!
God gives us laughter.
He gives us
a reason to laugh
and rejoice!
(Sermon III, 9)

Two things must be committed to memory:
humility and poverty.
Happy is the one
who carries these marks
in his mind
and in his hand,

who bears witness to them
and acts accordingly.
And so he will find:
the faltering wisdom,
the feeble power,
the meek grandeur,
the immeasurable small,
and the rich impoverished:
in a stable lays the one
who presides
over the realm of angels!
The hay of the beasts of burden
is the fare of angels!
The one whose name is boundless
is laid in the narrow manger.
(Sermon III, 10)

The Theology Professor: Saint Francis Appoints Anthony

The examples that address the mystery of the Incarnation
have been chosen with a specific purpose in mind. For here
the logic by which God offers his love to humankind
becomes tangible. This logic of God, or we might say, the
"theo-logic," was what Francis of Assisi wanted to discover
and grasp with all of his senses in the crèche celebration at
Greccio in 1223. When he heard about the power of
Anthony's oration and his deeply rooted theology, he
appointed him as the first theology professor of his commu-

nity. This was, for the time, quite an impressive move for Saint Francis, who was known to disdain any form of theological or scholastic superiority. In fact, in 1220, in an uncontrolled moment of anger, Francis cursed Brother Peter Stacia, a brother who had formerly been a professor of law, for building a large study house for the brothers. In contrast, Francis seemed to have no reservations about accepting a man like Anthony as professor. Nevertheless, Francis probably became convinced at some point of the necessity for study. At the same time, though, Francis laid down very clear stipulations for teaching to which Anthony was expected to adhere, as indicated in his appointment letter.

Fortunately, the appointment document survived. Since it referred to the Rule that was authorized on November 29, 1223, it had to have been written at the beginning of 1224. The letter to Anthony read: "Brother Anthony, my bishop: I, Brother Francis, send you my greetings. It is my pleasure that you preach the holy theology to the brothers, provided you do not extinguish the spirit of prayer and devotion as it stands in the Rule."

For many this letter was initially perceived as disappointing, because it contained nothing to indicate a closeness, intimacy or friendship between the two saints. There was nothing that led one to the conclusion that the addressee and the author had a close relationship.

Only the salutation was cause for puzzlement. Bishop? Anthony was not a bishop, but rather a simple priest. The designation, "bishop" must come from Francis, and early sources, including Thomas of Celano, confirmed this (Works, 1999). Moreover, a forger would not have written such a statement unless he wanted to be exposed as one. So what did Francis mean when he called Anthony "bishop"? Did he mean it in an ironic or humorous way? If so, one is left to wonder if Francis was saying, "Anthony, you are acting like a bishop in Romagna! Please, be first and foremost a true lesser brother. Show what you can do inside the brotherhood as well, by teaching the brothers a proper theology."

Or was it more probable that Francis melted in respectful distance? Francis had the same attitude toward theology as toward the Word of God itself or toward the Eucharist. This theology stated that the Word of God, the priest, and the Eucharist was one intrinsically connected entity. Without a theology, which gives the gift of "spirit and life," no word had an effect: without the Word, there was no Eucharist, and without the Word there was no priest and vice versa. In addition, the fourth Lateran council, which was held in 1215, impressed on bishops the importance of proclaiming the Word of God, either themselves or through others. In keeping with this proclamation, it was likely that Francis actually meant: "You stand so closely in the service of bishops, and have so much success that you are entitled to the honorary title of bishop."

Anthony's Theological Method

The permission Francis gave was nonetheless dependent on certain conditions: the theology taught must respect and encourage the personal relationship of the students with God and the spirit of prayer; and it must deepen the perspective of the Franciscan way of life, which has at its core total devotion.

But what theology was meant? Certainly a continuous and methodical reading of the Bible was a fundamental element. From two sources we have more precise information about the methods Anthony used. He used the method he learned in Coimbra that reflected the exegesis method, or the normal method of church scholars, which specifies four interpretive steps.

The first step involved an understanding of the historical meaning of a text; the actual intention of why a specific passage was written. The etymology of the words and names was more important to Anthony than the historical circumstances surrounding a specific passage or the historical events described in the text.

The difference between the historical-critical and etymological methods can be best illustrated with an example. In the gospel of Luke, the name Caesar Augustus appears in the well-known passage describing the circumstance at the time of Jesus' birth. Modern exegetics would ask who this emperor was and how he is seen from a biblical point of view. They would talk about his power that spanned the world, about the peace he imposed, about his questionable law of counting the inhabitants. In the Bible the census was criticized as one of a leader's most serious offenses (2 Samuel 24; 1 Chronicles 21). A truly historical reading of the Christmas story would have to show the inconsistency at that time between an emperor who wanted to secure and have control over his people by means of a census, and the child for whom there was no room in the inn. For Anthony, however, who looked to etymology for support, Caesar was *the one who retains possession* and Augustus *the venerable one*. Emperor Augustus therefore stood for God personally, who *enacts his decree* through preachers in order to impel people to seek forgiveness and penance, as well as to establish his rule through the prelates. The outer world was not a subject of consideration in such an exegesis; the biblical critical viewpoint of such a decree was not even recognized. What finally remained was a religion that served to support the Church and social order. It would be a mistake to assume that this meant a religion responsible for human dignity. A religion of the Incarnation, of intervention in the real world, was not even hinted at. The outer world was not a subject of consideration in such an exegesis; the biblical critical viewpoint of such a decree was not even recognized. In fact, the work Anthony quoted most often was the Etymology of Isidor of Seville—further striking evidence of his scholarship. His comprehensive knowledge was documented as well in countless quotations by the Church Fathers and philosophers and through his extensive knowledge of manuscripts.

The second step required the text to be examined for "what gives support to faith," as Anthony himself said. Scriptures, therefore, were to be understood as the language of God, and the reader or listener, who was also the person of faith, needs to enter into this dialogue with God.

The third interpretive step was the recognition that the text changed one who read it. Anthony's method was one of engagement or as he put it, one should be able "to impress itself upon principles and to penetrate resolve with its sweetness."

The fourth and final step was to bring about the full effect of a text by showing how the text "is joined to the fullness of joy and the blessedness of angels," and how the text and one's interpretation of it is connected to the heavens, into the future and beyond. This connection with the text is in fact the first sense of God, Anthony believed, which is felt here on earth.

Anthony as Theology Professor

Instituting these methods in all of his orations, Anthony carried out his function as theology professor (in study halls, not universities), though only for a short time, in Bologna, Toulouse, Montpellier and finally in Padua.

During his preaching missions, Anthony distinguished himself through his openness to new ideas in the area of theology. Evidence of this was found in the *Raymundina*, another account of Anthony's life from the thirteenth century, which claimed that he and Adam of Marsh, who was also a Franciscan and one the greatest theologians of the thirteenth century, studied the works of Saint Dionysius, a theologian who had a fundamental impact on western theology. One of the most important representatives of the "godly teaching" of Dionysius at that time was the Abbot of Vercelli, Thomas Gallus. Anthony attended several of his lectures, and a close friendship developed between them. Thomas Gallus later wrote in a report: "Brother Anthony of the Friars Minor, my good friend, strove to learn mystical theology. He made such good progress toward this end that I can say of him what was said of John the Baptist: he was a bright light that shined outwardly through his good example."

As a theology professor Anthony enjoyed the trust of the order as well as the church. Therefore, when the first problems with interpreting the Rule following the death of Saint Francis arose, the Franciscans called upon Anthony for his help and guidance. For example, the General Chapter of May 25, 1230, was unable to come to agreement on the interpretation of Francis' Rule and many of the brothers requested papal intervention. As a result, the Pope called upon a commission of experts, made up of highly qualified brothers, including Anthony of Padua, to interpret the Rule. Ultimately, the commission decided upon the papal explanation of the Rule, *Quo elongati* of September 28, 1230. Again, Anthony of Padua was present and played a very important role in the procedure and, ultimately, the history of the

Franciscan Order; once again exemplifying his theological authority, not to mention his devotion to the Rule as well as the followers of Francis of Assisi.

In the background of this counsel, a friendly relationship developed between him and Gregory IX, who mentioned during the canonization process that he knew Anthony personally: "We knew firsthand the holiness of his life and his wonderful behavior, for he lived a time among us." Gregory would also call him the *Ark of the Covenant* or *Treasure Chest of the Promise* and sounded the first note to herald him as Doctor of the Church (although Anthony would be first recognized as such by Pius XII, who would give him the title, *Doctor of the Scriptures* on January 16, 1946).

In 1228 Anthony gave a sermon before the papal court and left behind a lasting impression. As a consequence, he was immediately commissioned by Pope Gregory IX to write a collection of sermons for all the Sundays and Holy Days in the year. Anthony began work on it at once and completed it within a two-year period. After this work was finished, the nephew of the pope, Cardinal Rainald, who later became pope himself, asked him to write a collection of sermons for the feast days of the saints. Unfortunately, Anthony was only able to finish half of it before his death in June 1231.

Anthony's collections of sermons, gathered in three thick volumes today, were simple, and most definitely lack the fiery language of Anthony's spoken word. Some sections contained in the collection came from his theological lectures and have an academic character in keeping with the time in which they were written, and probably did not fill any listener with much fervor. Nevertheless, the teachings of Saint Anthony in this great work continue to speak to generation after generation. Rich treasures lay buried in these texts, particularly in the areas of spirituality and mysticism.

Anthony and Saint Francis

Anthony's place in Franciscan history was of great importance. Individual aspects of his work as an expert for the interpretation of the Rule cannot truly be estimated in terms of the time devoted to it nor the content itself. But we can assume that the scope of these areas was great indeed.

Already, we have presumed that there was no real acquaintance, much less a friendship, between Francis and Anthony. One may conjecture that they simply had too little time to form a friendship. Or one might presume that they were also fundamentally two different types of people and therefore friendship would have been unlikely. Nevertheless, as Franciscans, one would expect that despite these differences, they would have had a special closeness anyway.

We know with certainty that Anthony saw Francis at the previously mentioned Chapter of 1221, but we don't know to what extent they interacted. One might also presume that Anthony's practice of passivity and silence may have prohibited him from interaction with other brothers, including

Francis. However, in 1223 and 1224, it became difficult for people not to take notice of Anthony. In fact, Anthony was "thrust" on Francis by the brothers from Bologna, who encouraged Francis to name Anthony theology professor.

At the same time, though, nowhere in the collected sermons of Saint Anthony does the name "Francis" or "Franciscans" appear. The "Franciscan" in Anthony's life was clearly not defined by the name alone. It was found much more in how he lived his life and in what he proclaimed.

Prior of the Order

As previously stated, in 1224 at the Chapter of the Franciscans in southern France, Anthony gave an impressive sermon, which left many to wonder, under what office did Anthony conduct this sermon? Was he given the responsibility to speak because of the fact that he was a fascinating speaker, or because it was part of his office in the community?

What remains certain was that Anthony carried out an office in the same year in Puys, where he acted as guardian, or as head of the household. He was not, according to Francis' wishes, allowed to interact with his brothers in the logic of power, but rather he was expected to act with the logic of true service and devotion. The brothers who were entrusted to his care experienced this completely as they were "watched over" (e.g., "guardian" thus being synonymous with "watchman") by Anthony. There in Puys, the brothers under Anthony's guardianship were therefore free to make themselves at home.

In 1226 Anthony became *custos* in Limoges. Custos is, in fact, a vague term, for which today we have a limited interpretation. The word signified something along the lines of "guardian." Anthony was expected to mobilize his guarding/protecting energy for his fellow brothers as a *custodire*, which meant to protect and care for. But this function probably extended to brothers in an entire region. Here, he built bridges of communication from community to community and organized a central arrangement for several local communities.

That same year was a decisive year in Franciscan history. On October 3, Francis died, his body marked by the wounds of the stigmata. The whole order was informed in a moving obituary written by Brother Elias. The death of their founder resulted in a meeting of the brothers on the following Pentecost in 1227 at the General Chapter in Assisi to decide on a new leader. To everyone's surprise this was not Brother Elias, as was expected, but rather Brother John Parenti.

Anthony of Padua's fate was also decided at this Chapter. There he became the provincial of Romagna, and was thus given responsibility for the entire region of Upper Italy. In this capacity he was required to visit each community and every single brother, and sensitively and attentively find out what best served the needs of the brother. It was primarily an office where encouragement and comfort were called for, new possibilities were uncovered, and where decision-making and leadership were required. In 1228 Anthony chose Padua as his place of residence; it was the city he came to feel closest to, and likewise the city that remained united with him in the same feeling of kinship.

In 1230 Anthony returned to Assisi again as the provincial for the occasion of the General Chapter when the remains of Saint Francis were brought from San Giorgio, the provisional resting place, to San Francesco. The solemn procession was disturbed when the crowds that gathered rioted and attempted to seize relics. As a result Francis' burial was then closed off to the public and held in secret. Unbeknownst to Anthony, who one might presume would be shocked by such a display, something similar would happen to his own burial as well.

The General Chapter, as noted previously, named Anthony to the commission of experts, who were to act as advisors to Gregory IX on the official ecclesiastical interpretation of the Franciscan Rule. The chapter brought him great freedom. Up until that point, Anthony was bound by many obligations: itinerate preacher, theology professor and prior of the order. The chapter recognized what Anthony truly felt was his calling and decided that from that time forward he would be permitted to serve solely as an itinerate preacher.

The freedom Anthony was granted at the General Chapter of 1230 resulted in an unforeseeable dynamic. He journeyed again from place to place where massive crowds flocked to see him. Anthony had no idea where these journeys might ultimately take him, but he knew inevitably they were leading him to his own spiritual highpoint: Heaven.

The Lenten Action of 1231

In 1231 Anthony came up with a Church-defining idea: Anthony made Lent a public event. Lent, he said was not only an individual act of retreating in silence, but also a collective time for the community, and for the whole city. Anthony mobilized the bishop, the cathedral chapter and a number of priests as well as the political leaders. Before this happened, however, Anthony received permission from the pope to do so (or it is presumed he would have been required to do so). Despite the physical strain it would put on Anthony's body, he nevertheless wanted to preach in a different church every day during the Lenten season so that the entire city could hear him. At the time Anthony was already severely afflicted with illness: asthma and dropsy, which caused severe swelling and often made it impossible for him live a normal life.

At the beginning of Lent he suffered from nightly attacks of near-suffocation, which in the oldest biographies of his life are not recognized as being in connection with his illness. According to these accounts the attacks were merely caused by the Devil, who slyly tried to strangle the defenseless Anthony in the middle of the night while he was sleeping. For those who are familiar with the medical cause it could have been a lung edema, or the result of his asthmatic condition. The account of his life said that Anthony overcame his breathing difficulty with a prayer to Mary and by making the sign of the cross. Though one might find this plausible, one might also attest that Anthony was not himself fully aware of the impact his disease had on his health.

Nevertheless, Anthony set out to accomplish the greatest achievement of his life: to be a model for all people during the Lenten season. In order to set a good example, he kept to a strict fast, eating only once a day and only a small amount. In its religious form, fasting was thought to bring about freedom, open new perspectives, and clear the way for the Word of the living God. Anthony himself partook in these results when he first fasted during meditative encounters, and he wanted to share this with the entire city.

Anthony saw himself as a servant of the Word. His sermons became quite a common occurrence in Padua and Anthony encouraged all who attended his sermons during Lent to do as he had done: he wanted everyone to visit a new church every day (at this time Padua had fifty-five churches), so that they would be better prepared to proclaim a heartfelt and liberated "hallelujah" in the cathedral on Easter.

Before long, it became increasingly evident that Anthony's grand plan and idea would not be able to be carried out to complete fruition: the churches were too small to hold the crowds of people who flocked to them. In order to accommodate his sermons, people were forced to gather in parks, the marketplace and the Roman theater (perhaps where the famous Chapel of Scrovegni stands today). It was said that at times, some 30,000 people gathered together.

Reports during that time period told of how people gathered for Anthony's sermons days in advance, how they brought their bedding with them, and how they set up camp for the night before the sermons for fear of missing something. As with modern-day celebrities, bodyguards always accompanied Anthony wherever he went. The bodyguards were often young men who were called on to protect Anthony from the pressing crowds of people, and to open a passage way through which Anthony could walk. Everyone wanted to touch him and whoever succeeded in doing so was considered blessed. Women even brought sharp objects with them in order to cut off a corner of his habit to take home with them as a souvenir.

Delivering sermons to large crowds was not all that Anthony did during this time either. Anthony was extremely busy. Indeed, Anthony began early in the morning with a sermon that was expected to have lasted around two hours, but immediately afterwards he and several other brothers gave consultation and heard confession. In addition, he went on visits and intervened in conflicts as a means to find peaceful solutions. Often he was even called on to arbitrate legislative and political matters. His day was frequently quite busy, and left little time for rest throughout the entire period of Lent and the Holy Week preceding Easter.

As a side note, Anthony believed that the sermon and the sacrament of penance were one entity. Whoever preached, he believed, should have this focus in mind. He believed that the listeners wanted to make a new start and should, therefore, receive a new perspective on life. They could do this, he felt, in two ways: they needed to be able to recognize their own error and they needed to desire God's forgiveness. Hearing confessions, then, was as important as giving lengthy sermons. One should note that Anthony must have received permission to hear these confessions, for it broke the customary practice of only being allowed to confess to one's own priest.

Beyond preparing the people of Padua for Lent, Anthony's Lenten action transcended many aspects of civil life. Anthony was able to bring peace between feuding families, political parties and public figures. Anthony was also instrumental in the release of several prisoners, for whom he helped to grant amnesty and a general pardon for certain crimes. He even brought about the draft of a law that prevented insolvent or debt-ridden people from being imprisoned, as noted here in a document date March 17, 1231: "At the request of the honorable brother, holy Anthony, father confessor of the order of Friars Minor, from now on no debtor or citizen may be robbed of his personal freedom when he is insolvent. In such an instance he may be held liable in terms of his possessions, but not in terms of his freedom." Anthony also felt great compassion for the prostitutes who were forced to sell themselves at the market, and sought to liberate them from their fate by helping them.

Anthony had a definite understanding of how to proclaim the Gospel. He did not limit himself to an inward understanding alone, but also knew that he was responsible for forming part of the world. As a preacher and theologian he was obligated to society, the world and history, rather than simply being the "groundskeeper of the gardens of individual souls."

Political Mission

Here we must pause to ask ourselves today what in fact religion actually means. Is religion something that runs parallel to reality; is it something isolated? Or is it precisely something that does not let itself be pushed into the sacristy or solely fixed in an interior life at the risk of losing, as so often is the case today, every power and aura? Religion is much more a certain attitude toward the entire reality, or to say it in another way: religion is the connection of the outer and inner world to the Incarnated God.

This idea was precisely what Anthony, the preacher and theologian, stood in service to—that the faith was everyone's way to reach the Incarnated God, and one must do so through many acts of service.

This was why he could not refuse the mission that the city of Padua entrusted him with at the end of the Lenten action. Even though he was close to exhaustion, he set out for Verona, where Ezzelino, a brutal and violent tyrant who ejected the previous ruler of the town, had set up his own rule. Anthony wanted to ask Ezzelino for the clemency of Count Rizzardo of San Bonifacio, the former ruler of the city of Verona, who was languishing in the prison there. Meanwhile, Count Rizzardo's family, relatives and friends were forced to flee to Padua.

In order to assess this mission, it was necessary to know that Ezzelino's brother, Alberich, who was just as brutal a tyrant himself, had taken control of the city of Vicenza. The concentration of power in the hands of the family had led to the foundation of the so-called Lombard League, which united Padua, Milan, Bologna, Brescia, Mantua, Treviso and Vicenza. Now through Ezzelino's intervention Vicenza had broken away from the League. Anthony's mission thus had an even greater significance. Ultimately it involved not only freeing Rizzardo, but also easing the tension in the relations of both blocks: the League and Ezzelino. But the mission turned out to be a complete failure. In the end Anthony did not accomplish anything. Four months later someone else managed to secure Rizzardo's freedom and shortly thereafter Ezzelino also gained control over Padua, which itself became a victim of violent acts of revenge.

In contrast to the historical reality, the later legend transformed the failure into a success and the ferocious Ezzelino was depicted as a Christian convert. In reality Ezzelino remained a brutal tyrant and died on October 1, 1269 in a Milan dungeon following ten years of imprisonment.

On the way home from his failed mission at the end of May 1231, Anthony paused for a moment on a hillside on the outskirts of Padua. He admired the gracefulness of the landscape and was captivated by the plateau before him. He sang a moving tribute to the city of Padua, a kind of *Canticle to the Sun* one might say. To the brother who accompanied him, Anthony said that the city would soon receive a great honor. These were puzzling words which in retrospect heralded his imminent death and the canonization that followed it. Indeed, Padua would be figuratively raised up to a higher level through Anthony. In his chronicle written toward the end of the century, Fra Elemosina observed "through his teachings and miracles Anthony made the town of Padua known throughout the world."

At the Top of a Nut Tree in Camposampiero

The Lenten action and failure in Verona had left their mark on Anthony. Anthony felt burned out and totally fatigued. Thus it was his wish to retreat to the quiet of a Camposampiero, approximately eight miles outside of the city of Padua. An influential count by the name of Tiso IV, who converted to the faith after hearing one of Anthony's sermons, gave the Franciscans a place to settle on his estate in Camposampiero. He built for them a hermitage where a small community of brothers led a life of prayer and devotion to God. It was there Anthony went to recuperate and at the same time to complete his work on the feast days of the saints. During Anthony's stay here, Tiso became a dear friend to Anthony.

One day while walking through the nearby woods Anthony stopped in front of a nut tree that he had noticed along the way. His heart was filled with wonder at its beauty. He could not stop gazing at the crown of the tree with its lush branches and leaves. Suddenly he had an idea: if he were a bird, this would be where he would build his nest. Already he was captured by the idea and there was no holding him back. This was where he also wanted to live!

As noted previously, trees held a special fascination for Anthony. In Udine he preached from a tree. The explanation for this fascination with trees given in the oldest account of his life is completely different than others I have read, namely that Anthony sought the top of trees because of his asthma ailment. Even if this played a role, his love for trees touched a deeper side of him.

In a sermon Anthony also reflected on the spiritual meaning of trees. He once quoted Isidor of Seville: "We call roots what sink deep into the ground and form an anchor to the earth. As biologists say, the deepness of the roots corresponds to the height of the tree. The trunk of the tree is what stretches upward out of the roots. The branches are what grow from the trunk; they are what leaves and fruit are suspended from." On the surface this seemed to be nothing more than an observation of nature. However, it was now elevated by Anthony to receive a fundamental and human meaning: "There are five elements which are essential: humility as the roots, obedience as the trunk, love as the branches, the holy Word as leaves, and sweetness of the highest contemplation as the fruit." The correspondence of these virtues and their sequence in relation to the different parts of the tree contained wisdom worthy of a closer look: "the deeper humility is rooted in the heart, the greater the deed. The higher the water rises the lower it recedes. False humility seeks to appear great in deed because its roots are shallow in the heart. True humility will be ever more humbled the deeper its roots extend, and then the greater it will be." Anthony continued with his reflection on the ten steps to humility. It was as if he first saw the roots when he looked at the crown of the tree, for they were the reason for such a mighty crown. Humility determined a person's true greatness. Thus, Anthony wanted to nest in humility—to give himself completely up to the God who humbles himself—to be able at the same time to celebrate his true greatness in God's mystery (Sermon I 562f).

Tiso, with whom Anthony shared his wish, built the nest for him personally. When it was completed and Anthony had taken his place in the crown of the tree he felt the breeze, and heard the rustle of the leaves in the wind. He sensed the roots and the trunk, and lived in the atmosphere he needed to transport him to heaven. Contemplation, the silent openness for the mystery of God, has also been compared to the flight of birds. Here he experienced the mid-point between the depths of humility and the heights of heaven. And at this time he also wrote his sermons. "In the cell in the tree," the oldest account of his life tells us, "the servant of God leads a heavenly life; as industrious as a bee he gives himself up to holy contemplation. This was his last domicile among the living, and so he showed us that by ascending he was nearing heaven" (Assidua 1984, 15:7).

He incidentally did not live alone in the tree, but two other brothers, Roger and Luke Belludi, were there as well, for Franciscan wisdom dictates that no one shall be left alone, neither in the hermitages nor on a preaching tour. At meal-times, signaled by the tolling of a bell, they climbed down from the tree and made their way to the nearby community.

Collapse and Death

On the day of Anthony's death, again he heard the tolling of the bell and climbed down from the tree to join his fellow brothers in the community. Even before the meal was finished Anthony collapsed. It was likely that he suffered a heart attack. The brothers led him out of the dining area and laid him on a stretcher. Shortly before his death, he had expressed the wish to be brought back to Padua, to his beloved cloister San Maria, where he had lived and worked. And so the brothers laid him in a rickety cart, pulled by a pair of oxen, and set out to Padua on the route parallel to the Musone

River, which after 1964 would be called the "Way of the Saint." Anthony's condition progressively worsened the closer they got to Padua. Near Arcella they met up with another brother who was just on his way to visit Anthony in Camposampiero. He joined them and the dying Anthony. In light of the situation, Brother Vinotus suggested stopping at the community of Franciscan brothers that was situated in the cloister of the Poor Clares in Arcella, instead of venturing on to Padua. Vinotus feared that there would be a civil uprising if they were to transport Anthony through the city.

Agreeing with Vinotus, the group stopped by the brothers in Arcella. The brothers heard the confession of Anthony, who received absolution and led them in a hymn to the Virgin Mary. Though the Anointing of the Sick was not considered necessary, as Anthony has already received inner anointment, he received the sacrament in memory of those in need. Anthony cried out, "I see my Lord!" and after praying all of the seven penitential Psalms, Anthony died; and in the poetic language of a legend, "his soul plunged into the chasm of light" (Assidua 1984, 17, 15). It was Friday evening, June 13, 1231.

Unfortunately, the church of Arcella is not in its original location today. In 1517 the Arcella cloister, located somewhat north of where the train station is today, was destroyed by the Republic of Venice as no strategic sites were tolerated near the city fortifications. When the saint's death is commemorated today it is therefore necessary to choose a substitute location, which expresses little of the original atmosphere. A church was, however, built on the place where Anthony had initially collapsed, and there was also a cell built that showed where Anthony was said to have had his vision of the Christ Child. In the fifteenth century a chapel was also built on the location of the nearby nut tree, which today is looked after by the Poor Clares.

4:
Saint Anthony's Legacy

Saint Anthony's legacy,
reflected in the works attributed to him following his death,
was not a linear continuation of his earthly life. This phenomena could be described as a leap, for at least outwardly
there was no direct connection between the fascinating
speaker and the miracle worker that he soon became in Padua
and throughout the whole world immediately following his
death.

Passion and Fervor and the Cult of the Dead
In connection with the amazing events immediately following
Anthony's death, the oldest account of his life told the reac-
tion of the population that had positive as well as negative

aspects, but the reaction, nevertheless, was one of "passion and fervor" (Assidua 22, 3).

Fearing civil chaos, the brothers wanted to keep Anthony's death a secret. But they were unsuccessful. Suddenly a group of children (no one knows how they learned about the death) swarmed through the city crying out, "The holy father is dead, holy Anthony is dead!" On hearing this, the people flocked to Arcella in droves. The inhabitants of Capo di Ponte, an important bridgehead at that time and a traffic junction where many key routes came together, stationed armed troops on the bridge above the Bacchiglione in order to protect the body of Anthony.

The city of Padua and entire region was in mourning, and soon many people began to stake their claim on the body of Anthony. For example, the Poor Clares, who were never able to see Anthony during his lifetime due to their strict cloistered existence, desired to be the home of Anthony's final resting place. The Poor Clares felt that it was the will of God that Anthony find his final resting place with them, and soon they united with the noble families of their city to try to make their wish a reality.

The Franciscans on the other hand did not want to accept that Anthony, who undoubtedly had the wish to be laid to rest in their cloister in Padua, should be buried in a strange place. They turned to the bishop who called for a meeting of the cathedral assembly. After intensive counsel he came to the conclusion that the rights of the brothers should be respected. To accomplish this, he commissioned the dynamic mayor, Stefano Badoer, a Venetian who had previously held this office from 1228–29 and had been re-elected for the years 1230–31, to order the placement of Anthony's body.

But the bishop's request was refuted during a council meeting of the community of Capo di Ponte, and the citizens decided to take up armed resistance against the Franciscans. The citizens swore on their life and property to stand by the decision that Anthony should remain in their district, and they prepared for anything.

Because Albert of Pisa, the responsible provincial of the Franciscans, was not present, the brothers wanted to wait before they took further action. The brothers from Arcella locked the doors and set up barricades against the threat of an attack. At midnight an agitated crowd of people who wanted to see the body of Anthony attempted a break-in. To the amazement of the brothers, the citizens broke all of the locks and bolts, but no one was able to push their way through to the body. Although the people were standing in front of the open doors, they were not able to even see inside to the place where the body was lying because of a blinding light that had filled the entire building. Later this would be included as one of the miracles that proved the holiness of the saint.

In the morning, even more people from far and wide had gathered there. They wanted to touch the body and when that was not possible, they removed windows and doors and took everything that wasn't nailed down as relics. A fiery sense for the religious, sacral and godly again revealed itself.

Because it was summer, the brothers feared that the corpse of the saint would soon begin to decompose. They decided to bury Anthony in a temporary grave. In great haste they laid Anthony's body in a wooden coffin and buried it in a shallow grave nearby. They were hardly finished when the cry went out: "They have taken the body away!" On hearing this, the crowd broke in and fought its way through to the place of burial. The ground was dug up but the coffin could not be located immediately. When it was finally located the people refused to believe the brothers who assured them that it was indeed Anthony's body inside. With a stake they hammered on the wooden box, but the sound of the hollow thumps did not provide them with any greater assurance.

Finally, the provincial arrived on Saturday evening. The citizens of Capo di Ponte demanded the body and showed him the written pact in which they had sworn life and limb to keep the body of Anthony there. Albert of Pisa answered: "By law you have no right to make demands, my dear people! If, however, you appeal to benevolence, then we are prepared to do what God will inspire us in the assembly of brothers. For the sake of peace and to show that I am no man of deception, I am in agreement that you watch over the body of holy Anthony until we make our decision."

One has the impression that Albert of Pisa struck the

right note. In any case it was a masterpiece of psychology: nothing was decided, everything was left open, even those who harbored completely contrary intentions were called into service.

On the third day, the Sunday following the death of the saint, at the wish of the provincial a council meeting took place in the city. The mayor decided that the place where Anthony had been laid to rest should be guarded and that no force should be used against the brothers. At the same time, he forbade the carrying of weapons so that an outbreak of violence could be avoided or at least kept under control.

On Monday the cathedral chapter met in order to achieve two aims: peace among the population and justice for the brothers. However, the lobby of the Poor Clares was so strong that the majority of the chapter was in favor of the body remaining in Arcella. Albert of Pisa spoke in the midst of this sensitive situation:

> I wish for peace with the nobility who are present here. But I have the impression that the arguments for justice and understanding do not carry the importance they should, for you are only driven by emotional considerations, while reason counts for nothing. I certainly acknowledge your enthusiasm, yet it is not marked by differentiated thought. Anthony was a brother of our order, you

cannot overlook that, and you could witness
with your own eyes that he was a member of
our community in all he did. That is why we
want to have the one with us who even during his lifetime chose his final resting place:
the Church of the Mother of God. Of course
you might say that he could not have chosen
his final resting place himself, because his
will, reflected in the strength of his obedience, was not free; only the superior has the
authority and freedom to make such a decision. Since I am that person I humbly ask
that what is based on law and reason should
be freely carried out.

The bishop weighed the arguments of both parties and took
the side of the Franciscans. He ordered that all subordinate
themselves to the will of the provincial Albert of Pisa. On the
fifth day following the death he decided that the entire cleric
should take part in a procession to Arcella. The bishop again
gave the order to the magistrate Stefano Badoer to see that
an orderly transfer of the body to Padua took place. Using
boats and other vessels he had an emergency bridge built on
the Bacchiglione, so they did not have to travel through
Capo di Ponte. However, the population heard of this plan
and through violent means destroyed the bridge as soon as it
was built. The city of Padua armed itself as well in advance.

Before long, the citizens of Capo di Ponte positioned themselves for battle in order to receive the troops of Padua.

This was all too much for the Franciscans as well as the Poor Clares. Both orders began to plead with the citizens of their respective cities, for they felt responsible for an imminent war. The Poor Clares conceded and agreed that the body of Anthony should be given back to the Franciscans. Everyone who had been a part of the violent destruction of the bridge was banned to the southern part of the city. In front of the assembled council, Stefano Badoer held a speech and placed them under oath: further resistance would be punished with a dispossession of all property. With this oath in place, Bishop and clerics as well as a vast crowd of people were free to now bring the saint back in a solemn procession to his home cloister to be buried in his final resting place.

The route that the solemn procession took on June 17th can be roughly reconstructed today, as it followed the course of a main road, the so-called *cardo-maximus*, an ancient Roman roadway. Then it continued by way of the Ponte Molino, today called the Via Dante, upward just about to the level of the cathedral where the Via Manin branched off to the left; on this street it proceeded further over the Piazza della Erbe and then straight ahead down the Via San Canziano, branching off to the right at the Via Roma. On this street the procession continued along until the Ponte delle Torricelle and then went straight ahead to the church, San Daniele. Here the street branched off leading to the area called "Ruthena," where at that time the little church of Saint Mary and the small Franciscan cloister which belonged to it stood. Here the Franciscans were finally able to lay Anthony to rest according to his wishes.

The "passion and fervor" surrounding the deceased Anthony continued to play a role throughout history, not only expressed in the various forms of popular piety, but also serious scholarship. Time and again (1263, 1350 and 1981) insatiable curiosity has been the motivating factor to open Anthony's grave, leading to the discovery that the entire skeleton had not decomposed and, to the astonishment of many, the tongue and vocal chords remained intact.

Today a massive church and cloister complex tower over the grave. The original little wooden church has since disappeared. It once stood where the Chapel of the Madonna Mora, or the Black Madonna is located. This chapel holds the sarcophagus of the Blessed Luke Belludi, the brother who witnessed Anthony's life and death. Between 1231 and 1263 the body of the saint himself was originally contained in this sarcophagus.

Miracles and Canonization

During his lifetime Anthony did not perform a single miracle. Only one event said to have taken place before his death was mentioned in the canonization process, and it was not necessarily interpreted as a miracle. According to the account, a man from Padua named Pietro was walking through the town one day with his four-year old daughter, Paduana, in his arms. She was not able to walk so he carried her everywhere. She also suffered from epilepsy. Along the way he encountered Anthony and held out the child to him, asking him to make the sign of the cross over her. Anthony obliged. At home when the father put the child down she was able to stand. He gave her a chair and a stick to support herself and she began to walk, at first with difficulty and then gradually better and better. At some point he was even able to take the stick away and she walked without any help. Also, the epilepsy never returned. Some might argue that it was not a miracle at all in that the father's belief led him to put his daughter down, where she could then stand on her own for the first time. Then a learning process or therapy ensued, which therefore provided a possible explanation for the healing.

However, immediately following Anthony's death, even along the way of the solemn procession from Arcella to Santa Maria, one miracle followed another and in the days and weeks following the burial, one also heard repeatedly of miraculous events. "Passion and fervor" was the psychological terrain that provided a natural breeding ground for the phenomena of healing.

The church officially recognized many incidents as miracles at the canonization. The oldest biography lists fifty-three altogether: the lame walked, the blind saw, the mute spoke, epileptics were healed, fevers subsided, the dead were brought back to life, the shipwrecked were rescued and many other extraordinary events took place. All the events were documented with names and places. It was as if exactly every kind of miracle and sign that happened in the presence of Jesus, and witnessed in the Gospels, took place then.

A collective movement was then set into motion and very different interest groups competed with each other to hasten the process of Anthony's canonization. The town council, cathedral chapter, university, Dominicans, members of other orders, the mayor, nobility and papal legate in Upper Italy all did everything possible in order to make sure Anthony was taken up into the host of saints and so that Padua, in their eyes, would emerge before the whole world as a kind of new Jerusalem.

Again and again delegations from Padua pressed Pope Gregory IX. He set up an investigation committee consisting of the Bishop of Padua, Jacopo Corrado, the Abbott of the Benedictines, Jordan Forzaté and the prior of the Dominicans, John of Vicenza (Jordan Forzaté and John of Vicenza were also later raised to the altar of holiness). During the final phase, the earlier Archbishop of Besançon and now Bishop of Sabina, Cardinal John, was asked to validate the documents from Padua. A commission of cardinals under the direction of Cardinal John of Abbéville was then to make a decision.

However, such a swift canonization was met with strong resistance by a number of cardinals. At the time the College of Cardinals consisted of sixteen members, who in all probability harbored a certain amount of animosity toward the Franciscan movement and expressed their resistance toward a further canonization of a Friars Minor, even though the canonization of Saint Francis had taken place roughly four years earlier. Also, the representatives of the Segni family (Pope Gregory IX, Rainaldo, who later became Pope Alexander IV, Ottaviano and Nicola) dominated such decisions, but were all known as being partial to the Franciscans. Rainaldo was, however, instrumental in preventing the all-too-swift canonization of Saint Clare, and it was thought he would act similarly in the case of Anthony. However, one of the cardinals, whose name is not known, had a disturbing dream that resulted in a shift of opinion in the College of Cardinals. Incidentally, this dream was interpreted as the intervention of Anthony himself. The final decision was reached on the Friday before Pentecost, May 28, 1232.

The actual canonization took place on Pentecost day, 1232 in the Spoleto Cathedral, not even a full year after Anthony's death. This was a record that only the Dominican Martyr, Peter, who was canonized on March 9, 1252, exceeded by two weeks.

The canonization at this time had five very distinct moments. First, there was the solemn address of the pope, in which the new saint was praised in every way possible before the assembled College of Cardinals, the bishop, the entire clergy and the general public. Second, the cardinal deacon read aloud the announcement of the officially recognized miracles (the oldest biography from the year of canonization indicates that all fifty-three miracles were named here). Third, the pope spoke the official canonization text; in this instance, the pope stated, "For the praise and glory of almighty God, Father, Son and Holy Spirit, the glorious Virgin Mary, the holy apostles Peter and Paul and for the praise of the holy Roman Church, we declare on the basis of the counsel of our brothers and other prelates that holy Anthony of Padua, who has been glorified by God in heaven and whom we honor on earth, is to be listed among the heavenly host of saints. His feast day shall be celebrated on the day of his death." The fourth step was the great prayer of thanksgiving (*Te Deum*) and the petitionary prayer. Here the saint's intervention would be called on. On this occasion Gregory IX said in the antiphon to the Church teacher: "Dearest teacher and light of the church, Saint Anthony, pray for our salvation." Finally, the solemn Pontifical Mass was held in honor of the new saint. From this time on Anthony was recognized as a miracle worker and Padua as a spiritual center, or new Jerusalem—a gathering place for pilgrims from all over the world.

Three years later, in approximately 1235, Julian of Speyer, who a short time before had gained recognition for a poetic work on Francis of Assisi, composed rhymed song texts intended for use in church service, in particular the famous *Si quaeris miracul.* This captured the whole world and had an important influence on the image of Saint

Anthony. The poetry and linguistic vitality of the Latin original are not adequately expressed in a translation, nevertheless, it reads:

> Seekers of miraculous power, behold:
> death, confusion, times of misfortune,
> evil spirits and leprosy flee,
> the sick rise up—healthy again!
>
> Oceans recede and chains fall off,
> lost members, lost belongings
> are asked for and received,
> by those young and old.
>
> Dangers pass by
> and misery has an end.
> Who learns of it must proclaim it.
> As they do in Padua!

Here for the first time one sees the motif—the image of Saint Anthony as the finder of lost things—that predominates in the twentieth century.

Stories and Legends

A look inside the churches and cloisters where Anthony is remembered shows an assortment of images that have evolved over time, though very few images are actually historically accurate. Nevertheless, the depiction of Anthony in the nut tree is perhaps an image that in fact corresponds closely to who he really was. Also, close to the historical truth is the image of the peacemaker of Padua, at whose outdoor sermon the people remained dry, despite a heavy rain shower. This scene was painted in 1509 by Gianantonio Corona in the "School of Saint Anthony," where the painting by G.Tessari depicting Anthony's death in Arcella was also found.

Most of the pictorial images do not reflect Anthony's life story, but rather the story of works attributed to him following his death. They do not wish to portray Anthony's own life as much as to record his legacy, which has Anthony's death, or rather his entry into heaven, as its starting point. These images want to touch the viewer on a personal level, and are meant to express healing and salvation. In the following section the most important stories and legends that made up Anthony's life have been captured, and, whenever possible, in the sequence they came into being.

The Unbreakable Glass
The story of the unbreakable glass was one of the stories presented in the canonization as a miracle. It involved a historical event following the burial of the saint in 1231, whereby it should be noted that similar stories were told in connection with other saints as well. According to the oldest biography, the following takes place: Aleardino of Salvaterra, a nobleman who since childhood had been a follower of the Cathari, did not believe that Saint Anthony was a man of holiness. In the presence of his family and an enthusiastic group of Saint

Anthony's followers, he took a glass drinking vessel and exclaimed: "If this glass I will now smash on the ground does not break, I will believe that Anthony is truly a saint." He then proceeded to hurl the glass to the ground. The glass remained completely intact. Aleardino converted, taking the unscathed glass with him to the brothers. He confessed his sins and became a Christian.

The Unbelieving Man

Another story documented in the canonization process told of the suicide attempt of a woman from Monselice. The woman attempted to "make her husband holy," meaning she wanted him to start to lead a religious life and go to confession. The man agreed to her wish, confessed his sins and as penance promised to accompany his wife on a pilgrimage to Santiago de Compostela. Soon afterwards they set out on the journey. The woman was content, even full of pride that she had succeeded in accomplishing the seemingly impossible. As soon as the man recognized her pride, he didn't want anything more to do with the pilgrimage to Santiago. The wife was angered and swore she would throw herself in the river if her husband did not stand by his promise. But the man did not budge from his decision, and so she threw herself in the river, but before doing so, she called on the help of Anthony. Immediately, she was swept away in the torrents. Several women who had observed the incident jumped into the water to save the woman. They were successful and the woman was pulled out of the water, not even wet.

In this story a tendency can be seen which is reflected in many of the miracle stories, namely to illustrate a specific verse from the Bible. In this case, "the unbelieving husband is blessed through the faith of his wife" (1 Corinthians 7:14).

The Drowned Boy

Following Saint Anthony's burial there were many cases of drowning victims being brought back to life. As documented in the canonization process from the oldest biography, a certain Domenico from the city of Comacchio went to work one day, accompanied by his son. They became separated from each other and Domenico later found the boy drowned in a lake. In a state of shock he carried the body home, where his wife made a solemn vow asking for Anthony's intervention. Soon afterwards the boy returned to life.

Often the revival of Anthony's nephew is the subject of paintings. It is a story which first originated in the fifteenth century: Parisius, the nephew, was playing with other children on a boat near Lisbon one day. The ship capsized and Parisius, unlike the other children, could not swim and he drowned. His mother, Saint Anthony's sister, heard the news and ran to the shore. Torn by grief, yet full of trust in Anthony, she initiated a search for the boy and vowed that Parisius would become a member of the order if he returned alive, which of course he did.

The Drowned Girl

The canonization process and oldest account of the saint's life also contain the story of the girl, Eurelia, who had apparently been dead for a longer time in the muddy waters of a river. It was clear that rigor mortis had already set in when the horrified mother found the body and took it out of the water. But the mother could not accept the girl's death. She made a vow to bring Anthony a wax votive offering if the child returned to life. The mother had hardly made the vow when the girl's body became warm with life again.

The Conversion of Ezzelino

Contrary to historical reality, which shows Anthony's mission to Ezzelino to be a complete failure, John Peckham reported in his biography, written between 1276–78, of the tyrant's miraculous conversion. After Ezzelino had once again caused a terrible bloodbath, Anthony, like Francis, placed himself directly in the den of the raging wolf. However, in contrast to Francis he assailed Ezzelino with sharp words in an aggressive tone. The effect was, however, the same. Ezzelino felt remorse, vowed to abandon his brutal ways and became as gentle as a lamb. Putting a rope around his neck, he threw himself at the feet of the saint and from that time on led a different life. He supposedly said, "In all truth I tell you I saw godly lightning come from the face of Father Anthony and strike me, so that I had the impression he was about to cast me into hell" (Peckham 1986, 17, 46). What was behind such a historical falsification? Could it have been the fear of failure? Or was it the pressure caused by the false conception of a saint who was expected to succeed at everything? Or was it simply the heartfelt wish for the wolf to be transformed? No one will ever know.

The Amputated Foot

Sometime during 1276–1278, John Peckham adapted the story of the amputated foot from Albertin of Verona, a Franciscan writer of sermons. One day Leonardo, a citizen of Padua (later legends would move the miracle to Spain), came to Anthony and confessed that he kicked his mother. Anthony responded passionately: "the foot that kicked the mother or father deserves to be cut off." Leonardo then goes home and cuts off his own foot. The news of this terrible self-mutilation soon reached Anthony, who turned to God in his reverence and devotion, and then hurried to Leonardo so as to, with God-given power, reattach the foot. This legend can clearly be identified as an illustration of the Bible verse: "If your right eye causes you to sin, tear it out and throw it away; it is better for you to lose one of your members than for your whole body to be thrown into hell. And if your right hand causes you to sin, cut it off and throw it away; it is better for you to lose one of your members than for your whole body to go into hell" (Matthew 5:29).

The Praying Donkey

The legend of the praying donkey has an interesting historical origin. A source from Franciscan circles related the following story. A Cathari fed his donkey with unconsecrated hosts. One day he argued with a priest who was faithful to traditional belief. The Cathari said, "My donkey eats a thousand hosts when they are given to her." The priest answers, "That's blasphemy! The Body of Christ is not food for donkeys, but food for souls. I will bring the Body of Christ to the donkey, if she eats it I will believe what you believe, if she doesn't eat it, then you must believe what I believe." When the priest returned with the consecrated host, the donkey knelt down and cried. The Cathari converted.

It is conspicuous that the person involved is an unnamed worldly priest, not even a Franciscan, no place name is given and the Cathari is also not named. This is a story that could be told everywhere and made to fit any location; in other words, a typical legend that has circulated by word of mouth from place to place.

In its connection to Anthony many different cities have been named as the location: Toulouse, Bourges, Limoges, Montpellier and Rimini.

John Peckham seems to be the first one who linked the story to Anthony and set it in Toulouse. Other sources claim a connection with Rimini. Because, as the life story of Anthony tells us, this was where the conversion of the "arch-heretic" Bononillus to Catholicism took place. The legend therefore serves to explain the unexpected conversion of such a well-known man.

According to Peckham's work, called the "Benignitas," the heretic said to Anthony: "Words are just words, let me see deeds! If you can prove with a miracle that the true body of Christ is present in the Communion of the faithful, I'll abandon my dogma and take up the Catholic faith" (Peckham 1986, 16,6). Anthony agreed to this. The Cathari continued, "I will lock up a donkey for three days and not give it anything to eat. Afterward, in front of all the people, I'll show it a pile of hay. You will stand there too, holding what you claim to be the Body of the Lord. If the starving donkey ignores the hay and kneels down without hesitation, then I will accept the faith of the church" (Peckham 1986, 16, 6). As expected, the donkey ignored the hay and fell on its knees in adoration. Bononillus was ashamed of himself, because what the donkey knew, he surely should have been able to recognize.

The Understood Language

John Peckham also related a story, described in greater detail in the 1330 *Deeds of Saint Francis and his Companions*. This legend was connected to historical facts in two ways. First, the problem still remained unsolved of how it was possible for a Portuguese native to make himself understood before such huge crowds of people in Upper Italy and in Southern France. It was of course possible that Anthony could have learned the vulgate, the Italian colloquial language that did not differ greatly from Latin, prior to his activity as itinerate preacher. But what about France? Was Latin or Italian understood there? Was the language difference there so small that he could be understood well? Or did Anthony have a translator at his disposal? There is, however, no mention of this in any of the sources. How then was he able to make himself understood? Was a new Pentecost necessary to make this possible?

The second point is the historic fact that Anthony was next to the Pope's home in Rome and probably had an opportunity to preach there. This international gathering place was a fitting stage for the legend that was intended to explain the language miracle of Saint Anthony. "Deeds" implies the gathering of a council, an assembly, or a consistory, but nothing more definite is known (John Peckham simply tells of a public sermon in front of pilgrims). In any case, there were those there who spoke Greek, while others were speakers of Latin, French, German, Slavic or English, and still others of different languages. Anthony gave a sermon and no one had any difficulty understanding him, which naturally led those present to ask: "Isn't he a Spaniard? How is it possible that each of us can understand him in our native language?" Pope Gregory IX declared: "truly this is the Ark of the Covenant, the keeper of the holy word!" The relationship to the Biblical miracle of Pentecost can clearly be recognized here, made tangible in the setting of Anthony's sermon.

The Vision of Luke Belludi

John Peckham reported that during the time of Ezzelino's reign of terror in Padua, when the entire population lived in fear and dread, Bartholomew de Corradino, the guardian of the cloister of Padua in 1256, kept watch and prayed. Suddenly he heard the voice of the saint say, "Do not fear, Brother Bartholomew, abandon your sorrow, have courage and rejoice; see that I have found mercy by God. On the octave of my feast the city will be conquered again and the freedom and independence of the past will be Padua's once again" (here we learn by chance that the celebration of Anthony's feast day lasted eight days). This would also happen. In pictorial depictions, however, the blessed Luke Belludi, Anthony's companion, and as the sources indicate, also Bartholomew's, is usually shown as the receiver of this vision (Peckham 1986, 23, 8f).

The Listening Fish

At the end of the thirteenth century someone invented the legend of the listening fish. Jean Rigaud, who wrote between 1300–1315, found the legend in written form and included it in his biography of Saint Anthony. He set the tale near Padua; other traditions placed it in Rimini, Venice, Ravenna, or Toulouse.

The location of Rimini, however, seems the most logical, because it was here that Anthony could not make headway initially. The Cathari held the town firmly in their grip. Only after a time was Anthony able to suddenly, and against all expectation, achieve a breakthrough. With Anthony's help, the city turned again to the Catholic doctrine.

But what was the cause of this miraculous transformation that came about as such a surprise? People needed an explanation, and so began the legend of the listening fish.

According to this story, Anthony pulled out all the stops. When the Cathari, the so-called pure ones, refused to listen to him, he went down to the sea and turned to the fish. He knew that for the Cathari the fish was a symbol of purity and holiness. Why shouldn't he then address the ones who were really pure, instead of those who regarded themselves as such but were not open enough to listen to him? And what a miracle it was! The fish gathered around in large numbers and listened intently. When the Cathari saw this they had no choice but to turn to the God who was in everything of flesh and of the earth. The satire of the famous Abraham of Santa Clara presented the event as follows:

> Anthony went to give a sermon
> But in the church there was no one,
> He proceeded to the river
> And preached to the fish there:
> > They beat with their tails
> > In the sunlight gleaming.
>
> The carp with roe
> They have all come friend or foe,

Their mouths opened wide,
To listen with delight:
 No sermon ever
 Had pleased the carp better.

Sharp-faced pike,
Otherwise scrounging,
Swim there in haste,
To hear the pious one speak:
 No sermon ever
 Had pleased the pike better.

And too every idealist,
Always at fasting,
The cod I believe,
To the sermon proceed:
 No sermon ever
 Had pleased the cod better.

Good eels and sturgeon
That the elegant dine on,
Trouble themselves here,
At the sermon to appear:
 No sermon ever
 Had pleased the eels better.

Likewise crabs and turtles,
Otherwise slow messengers
Rise in haste from watery ground

To hear this pleasing sound:
        No sermon ever
        Had pleased the crabs better.

Fish big and small,
Elegant and common,
Raise their heads,
With an understanding fire
        To fulfill God's desire
        And listen to Anthony.

The sermon ended,
No one had repented,
The pike remain thieves
The eels still conceited
        No sermon ever,
        Had changed them for the better.

The crabs return,
The cod remain fat,
The carp overeat,
The sermon forgotten.
        No sermon ever,
        Had changed them for the better.

The Poisoned Meal

Jean Rigaud also told the legend of the poisoned meal. Somewhere in Italy, the Cathari invited Anthony to a meal.

Following the example of Christ who dined with sinners, he accepted the invitation in the hopes of winning them for Christ. But they set a poisoned meal before him, with the announcement that they would return to the Catholic faith if he survived. Anthony made the sign of the cross over the plate and ate without the slightest harm coming to him. And so the Cathari returned to God. But things were not always done so openly. Another time, the Cathari made a secret attempt on his life. They served a poisoned meal to Anthony without him knowing it. Anthony made the sign of the cross over it and remained unharmed. This legend correlates to the Bible verse: "If they drink any deadly thing, it will not harm them" (Mark 16:18). Such a story was also told, for example, about Saint Benedict, who envious monks tried to poison.

The Heart of the Miser

This legend originated at the end of the thirteenth century and was an illustration of the Bible verse: "for where your treasure is, there also will your heart be" (Matthew 6:21). It was first found in a sermon collection long attributed to Saint Bonaventure, and was told more precisely than the later Saint Anthony legend. The pseudo-Bonaventure tale told of a bishop who, with respect to this verse, refused to give a miser a church burial and told his relatives to look for the man's heart in his own treasure chest.

At the beginning of the fourteenth century the Bible verse would be chosen as the maxim for an encounter between Anthony and a userer and written on a church stained glass window. Anthony indeed took usury to task. In 1231 he established the famous law intended to protect the victims of usury. But the legend had still not been born. In the second half of the fourteenth century, approximately 1385, Bartholomew of Pisa established a clear connection with Anthony. He told how on the occasion of a userer's funeral Anthony mentioned the Bible verse in his sermon. Anthony dared to claim that the man did not have his heart inside his body, but rather in his treasure chest. A check following the sermon proved that Anthony was right, for the userer's heart was discovered inside the treasure chest.

The Paternity Claim

The paternity claim was a legend that was said to have happened during Anthony's service in Ferrara in 1228. But it was not written until the second half of the fifteenth century. Sicco Polentone of Padua told the following story: A woman was forced to suffer from the uncontrollable jealousy and continual accusations of her husband. He accused her of being unfaithful, and even claimed that their last child was not his. Anthony intervened and instructed the child, who was not yet able to speak, to tell them loudly and clearly who his father was. The child did this, and the man's distrust and jealousy disappeared. The liturgy of the saint contained an antiphon that provided a commentary to this story: "Perfect praise flows from the mouth of infants." A connection was also made to the verse from scriptures: "Out of the mouths of babes and infants you have drawn a defense against your foes, to silence enemy and avenger" (Psalm 8:3; Matthew 21:16).

The Stabbed Woman

In approximately 1450 Sicco Polentone also told the story of the hot-tempered nobleman, who rushed to Anthony in Arezzo one day to confess that he had mistreated his wife in a fit of anger. He had stabbed her with a knife, and in fact so badly that she was likely to die as a result. Anthony went with him into his house and a short time later the woman was healthy again.

The Opening of the Tomb

Bartholomew of Pisa reported between 1385 and 1390, of an unofficial opening of Anthony's sarcophagus in 1350. According to this source, which however cannot be judged as completely conclusive, Cardinal Guido of Montfort separated the jaw from the head in order to have it set as a relic. The recounting of the events by Bartholomew Montagna in 1512 hardly differed from the photographically documented account of the grave opening ceremony in 1981.

The Ring

In the first quarter of the sixteenth century a picture was painted in Camposampiero that can barely be deciphered today. It depicted the legend of a lost ring, which through Saint Anthony's intervention, was recovered in a fish. Such circulated legends are still repeated with slight variation.

The Dead Man's Testimony

A Portuguese source from the sixteenth century told of the legend of the revival of a dead man, said to have occurred during Anthony's lifetime. Two citizens from Lisbon bore a strong animosity toward each other. In the darkness of night one of the men stabbed the son of the other. It was later added that the incident took place near Anthony's birth house. In order to draw suspicion away from himself, the murderer brought the body to the garden of Anthony's family. When the body was found, Anthony's father, Martin, was arrested on suspicion of murder and sentenced to death. Anthony heard of it and awakened the dead man to life, so he could reveal the identity of the real murderer and prove the innocence of his father.

Book, Flame, Heart, Lily, Cross and the Christ Child

There are many symbols or attributes that are used as a means to identify Saint Anthony. The first attribute was the book. The book was the oldest symbol to be featured with Saint Anthony. Its meaning was clear, based on what Anthony was: a preacher, a scholar and a theologian. But, Anthony was not only a scholar and man of reason, he was also a person of flaming love. The flame was an often-used symbol for this fervor. When Agnolo Gaddi was commissioned in 1394 to paint Anthony together with Saint Bonaventure, another theologian and man of letters, he gave Anthony the attribute of a burning flame. For approximately 150 years it remained the favored symbol in which to represent Saint Anthony. Similar to the flame, the heart had a like shape and meaning and was therefore transferable in depictions of the saint. Anthony's purity has often been symbolized by the depiction of a lily since the fifteenth century. Additionally, as it was with so many other saints, including Saint Francis, Anthony was often seen with a cross. Lastly, the Christ Child was the attribute seen most often, and is still popular today. The manifestation of the Christ Child was simply associated with the saint sporadically. Based on a source from the fourteenth century it was used sparingly, but by the seventeenth century the depiction of the Christ Child was always associated with the saint.

The Divided Bread
In the "School of Saint Anthony" the great artist Titian painted a motif in 1511 that is among the best known today. The painting depicted Saint Anthony, the guardian of the brotherhood, breaking bread. Anthony was therefore seen as the great helper in need, expressed symbolically in the breaking of bread.

Only later would the "Anthony bread" become a stereotypical image. On August 12, 1890, Louise Bouffier, a woman from Toulon, tried to open a door. Neither she nor a locksmith, who had been called to her aid, was successful. Louise Bouffier then called Anthony to help her, promising to take up the cause of the poor. She was suddenly able to open the door. In her thankfulness she placed a poor box in front of a statue of Saint Anthony, standing in her shop. With time a great deal of money was collected for the poor and the idea quickly spread. This devotion to Saint Anthony ultimately found its way to churches throughout the world.

Scientific Curiosity

Saint Anthony continues to intrigue us today. Even science isn't immune to the mystery and life of Saint Anthony, especially when it comes to examining the bones of the saint. The scientific examination in 1981 involving the examination of the well-preserved skeleton is summarized as follows:

> The skeletal structure shows no special anomalies and contains no indication of a specific illness. However, here and there physical traces can be ascertained which indicate habits of prayer, such as strict penitential practices that could have had an influence on the cause of death. The body measurements of Saint Anthony of Lisbon present a picture that differs from that found in art: he was approximately 1.70 meters (5 feet, 1 inch)

tall, his head had a longish form, his face shape was accordingly narrow; he had deep-set eyes, long hands and slim fingers; his stature was strong and well-proportioned: a typical person of the Atlantic-Mediterranean region. The age of the saint can be estimated as approximately forty; all evidence gleaned from various methods indicate this number to be more precisely thirty-nine years and nine months.

With this information the date of birth would have to be set back to the year 1191, from the original recorded date of 1195. Therefore the question can be raised of whom to believe: those who calculate the date of birth based on textual sources, or those who base their supposition on technological methods. In either case, Saint Anthony's legacy can be traced back to the mortal Anthony.

Summary

The story of Anthony's legacy, as with most legacies, is quite different than his actual life story. But perhaps there is a similarity after all? Isn't Anthony, the preacher and theologian, the physical expression of the word and language of the Scriptures, God's Good News? Wouldn't it therefore be justified to associate the promise of the Scriptures with him? The Word proclaimed should not simply remain the Word, but it should create a new reality. And so the new reality appeared, awakened to life through the Incarnated Word and reflected in the miracles of the man who would one day become a Doctor of the Church—Saint Anthony of Padua. The same saint who came out of the shadows to spread the Word resounds in the world where the kingdom of God is experienced in all its fullness to this day.

Prayer to Saint Anthony

> Saint Anthony,
> Intercessor before God:
> Pray and beseech,
> Request and thank—
> call with us in
> the mystery of God.
> Take up the cry,
> that comes from our need,
> carry it for us
> into the heart of God!
> Penetrate for us
> the ear of God,
> who holds everything in his hands,
> and do not cease
> until he turns his face to us,
> and helps us in our need.
>
> Saint Anthony,
> Helper in need:
> find what has been lost.
> Inflame man and woman in love:
> bind lovers,
> embrace the married.
> Hear the cries of the childless,
> ban the fear of the pregnant,
> dispel the pain of those in labor.

Drive away our fear of the future.
Awaken creative power
in society and the Church.
Give everyone work
that brings happiness.
Look after children, protect the elderly.
Feed the hungry, clothe the naked.
Give strangers shelter and a bed,
And everyone an open heart. Amen

Blessing Of Bread

God
hold your hand
over the bread we bake
over the bread we share
over the bread we eat.

Breathe life into it,
so death recedes.
Touch it with your love,
so it multiplies in our hands.
Bless it with your power,
so it becomes a feast.
This we ask through the intercession
of Saint Anthony
through Christ our Lord. Amen

Literature Cited

____. *The Life of Holy Anthony Told by a Contemporary.* Padua: 1984.

Bigaroni, Marino and Boccali, Giovanni, ed. *The Deeds of Saint Francis and his Companions.* Poziuncola: Jacques Cambell Contesto dei firoetti a fronte, 1988.

____. *Dialogue.* Padua: 1985.

Julian of Speyer. *Reimoffizium: The Second Biography.* Padua: Vergilio Gambosa Padova, 1985.

Peckham, John. 1278. *Benignitas.* Padua: 1986.

____. *Raymundina.* Padua: 1992.

Rigaud, Jean. *Rigaldina.* Padua: 1992.

Riva, C.; A. Rosmini, *The Five Wounds of the Church,* Critical edition. Paderborn, 1971.

____. The Sermons of Saint Anthony I. Padua: 1979.

____. The Sermons of Saint Anthony II. Padua: 1979.

____. The Sermons of Saint Anthony III. Padua: 1979.

Works, Francis; J.A. Wayne Hellman; William J. Short; and Regis J. Armstrong, eds. *Francis of Assisi: Early Documents: The Saint.* New York: New City Press, 1999.

Explanation of Literature Cited

1. The oldest biography from 1232, called *Assidua* or *Fervent Prayer* after the first word of the biography, was written with relative certainty in the year of the canonization by an unknown Franciscan. In great haste the author strove to record the effect of the saint's legacy on Padua; therefore showing how Anthony raised Padua up to a new Jerusalem. Not only are there large gaps between 1222 and 1228 in the biography, but it also lacks the focus on the qualities that define Anthony as a Franciscan.

2. The double volume by Julian of Speyer: *Reimoffizium: The Second Biography*, written in approximately 1235, was intended for the liturgical and clerical needs of Franciscans. The Padua-focused text was supplemented by the universal perspective of the Parisian study center with which Julian was associated. At the same time, Anthony's Franciscan qualities are emphasized.

3. The *Dialogue* was written in the years 1245–46 by an unknown author based on the model of Gregory the Great. The work contains a total of 259 miracles performed by Franciscan saints or members of the order perceived as holy. Out of these, 44 miracles are attributed to Saint Anthony. The miracles are integrated in various, fundamental reflections, presumed to have originated from the teaching work of the author, but firmly based on spiritual tradition. The work is structured so that a dialogue develops between "nar-

rator" and "listener." It is important to the author that readers do not get lost in the sea of miracles, but react sensibly, discovering a true help for their faith.

4. The *Benignitas* was written with relative certainty between 1276–1278 by the English Franciscan, John Peckham, and named after the first word at the beginning of the legend "The Good and Benevolent God has Appeared." Internal criteria showed the author to be a person who remained a stranger to the Italian culture, but nevertheless placed a great deal of emphasis on the Italian Anthony of Padua and Upper Italy. Additionally, Portuguese witnesses also gave him supplementary information. His primary matter of concern was to show the presence of God not only in Jesus, but also in people such as Francis and Anthony.

5. The *Raymundina* was written in approximately 1239 by an unknown Franciscan in Padua. The name came from the French Franciscan, Pierre Raymond of Saint-Romain, who was formerly seen as the author of the legend. Like the *Assidua*, the *Raymundina* was a legend that served the needs of the Franciscans of Padua and also reflected the contemporary situation.

6. The *Rigaldina*, named after its author the French Franciscan Jean Rigaud, was written between 1300-1315. As expected, much information was given regarding Saint Anthony's time in France. Jean Rigaud was a highly

acclaimed author of many works. His biography of Saint Anthony was not only written to encourage devotion to the saint, but also as a poetic counterpart to the concrete reality in which the Franciscan order found itself at this time: a new heaven, a new earth, a new human being.

7. *The Deeds of Saint Francis and his Companions* was written in approximately 1330. This work does not only deal with Saint Anthony but, as the title indicates, the entire Franciscan order. Chapters 44 and 45 concentrate on Saint Anthony. The intention of this work is not historical but spiritual. It seeks to place the miraculous before the historical and thus inspire the reader with a sense of the divine.

8. The Chronicles of the Friars Minor Brothers Jordan of Giano and Thomas of Eccleston contains information about the Chapter of 1221.

9. *The Works of Saint Anthony I and II* consist of the collection of sermon materials for Sundays and holidays and were written at the request of Pope Gregory IX, in the years 1228 and 1230.

10. *The Works of Saint Anthony III* contain the collection of sermon materials for the feast days of saints and were written at the request of Cardinal Rainald and partially completed by 1231.

Miscellaneous Sources

Clasen, S. *The Legend of Saint Francis*. Leiden, 1967.

Esser, K. *Beginnings and Initial Objectives of the Order of the Friars Minor*. Leiden, 1966.

Fabbretti, N. *Brother Anthony, the Restless Saint*. Salzburg, 1986.

Felder, H. *The Miracle of Saint Anthony According to the Older Sources*. Paderborn, 1933.

Gamboso, V. *La basilica del Santo di Padova*. Padua, 1991.

Gamboso, V. *Per conoscere S. Antonio*: La vita-il pensiero. Padua, 1992.

Gasparini, M. *Il santuario del noce in Camposampiero*, Padua, 1991.

Hardick, L. *"He came to you, that you might come to him"*: *Sketches of the Life and Teachings of Saint Anthony of Padua*. Werl, 1986.

Holter, B. *"To serve in a special service"*: *Francis of Assisi's Perspective on the Office of Priesthood and the Indications of his Diaconate in the "Opuscula"*. Werl, 1992.

Il ritorno del Santo. Ricognizione ed esposizione del corpo de S. Antonio nel 750 anniversario della morte (1231-1981). Padova, 6 gennaio-1 marzo, 1981. Padua: 1993.

Kleinschmidt, B. *Anthony of Padua in Life and Art, Cult and Popular Devotion.* Düsseldorf, 1931.

Kröger, F.J. *Saint Anthony Devotion.* Werl, 1991.

Lazzarin, P. *Un Santo - una basilica - una citta. Storia e segreti di un santuario notissimo e poco conosciuto - Virtu e vizi di una piccola granda citta,* Padova, 1990.

Meneghelli, V. and Poppi. *Ricognizione del corpo di S. Antonio di Padova.* Studi storici e medicoantropologici, Padova, 1981.

Nigg, W. *Anthony of Padua.* Freiburg, 1981.

Orati, D. *Storie antoniane nelle Rigioni d'Italia,* Padua, 1992.

Poloniato, L., ed. *A te Signore la loda. Preghiere di S. Antonio.* Padua, 1985.

Scandaletti, P. *Anthony of Padua: Saint of the People and Doctor of the Church.* Graz, 1983.

Schlager, P. *Saint Anthony of Padua in Art and Legend.* Mönchengladbach, 1923.